Yippee! It's Eid-ul-Adha

by

Farjana Khan, Ph.D.

AuthorHouse™
1663 Liberty Drive
Bloomington, IN 47403
www.authorhouse.com
Phone: 833-262-8899

Because of the dynamic nature of the Internet, any web addresses or links contained
in this book may have changed since publication and may no longer be valid. The views
expressed in this work are solely those of the author and do not necessarily reflect the
views of the publisher, and the publisher hereby disclaims any responsibility for them.

This book is printed on acid-free paper.

ISBN: 978-1-4817-0423-6 (sc)
      978-1-4817-0424-3 (e)

Library of Congress Control Number: 2012924399

Print information available on the last page.

Published by AuthorHouse   02/27/2021

authorHOUSE®

This book is dedicated to my beloved uncle Luthfer Belal Tarafdar. It is also dedicated to Anwara Khan, Faruque Khan, Feruza Khan, Michael Khan, Aleena Ahmed, Feruze Khan and other good-hearted family members. May God accept all their good deeds, including this book that will raise everlasting awareness.

In addition, thanks to all the individuals that were there for me one time or another: Nicole Murphy, Sarah Elfani, Hadil El Wahidy, Latisha Wright, Dora Danner, Lisa Lamb, Kapua Sawyer, Praveen Chopra, Henin Hidalgo, Russell Khan, Kathy Khan, Aniysah Cooper Starling, Ahsan Choudhury, Shimu Ahmed, Afreen Ahmed, Fauzia Khondker, Asha Ramlogan, Maria Ielati, Laurie Campanaro, Nadira Ahmed, Tracy Laumenede, Murshed Khan, Carina Summers, Ana Cruz, Omar Ahmed, and all my other cousins and friends.

'Twas the night before Eid-ul-Adha. Mom and I begin to prepare for the big day.

2

My brothers enter the room carrying trays filled with delicious food for tomorrow's celebration. Dad begins to call family members and friends to invite them over for Eid dinner. My dad then shouts excitedly, "I'm so glad it's Eid-ul-Adha tomorrow!"

Next, my sister plays Islamic nasheeds on the stereo while my brothers clean the house.

4

As the night continues, all the girls put on henna.
We finish cooking and go to bed.

In the morning, we go to the mosque to pray.

My mother gives money to people in need.

My father then goes to buy fresh goat meat for family members and the needy.

8

Afterwards, we visit our family and friends to give them goat meat and other presents.

9

At night, family members and friends come to my house for Eid dinner. We eat haleem and kebab. Dad reminds us that we celebrate Eid-ul-Adha to honor Prophet Abraham's act of sacrifice.

Then we all play games and tell jokes. As the night finally comes to an end, we remember all the things we are grateful for, the sacrifices we made, and the good work we've done. Everyone smiles with joy. Yippee! It's Eid-ul-Adha.

Author's Note

Eid-ul-Adha (a.k.a. the Feast of Sacrifice) is a Muslim holiday that honors Prophet Abraham's act of sacrifice. Eid-ul-Adha falls on the 10th day of the Islamic month called Thul Hijjah. Since Eid-ul-Adha follows the lunar calendar, it is observed approximately 10 or 11 days early each year. Eid-ul-Adha is also celebrated during the same month when Hajj takes place. Hajj is the annual pilgrimage to Mecca in Saudi Arabia. Muslims must go to Hajj at least once during their lifetime, unless they are sick or have financial difficulties.

Allah (SWT) tested Prophet Abraham (may Allah be pleased with him) by commanding him to sacrifice his first-born son Ismael. As Prophet Abraham was about to sacrifice his son, Allah (SWT) put a ram in front of him instead. Hence, the prophet sacrificed the ram instead. The fulfillment of this command of Allah emphasizes Prophet Abraham's obedience and faith in Allah.

On this special day, Muslims wear new clothes and attend Eid prayer. Families also visit each other and enjoy delicious meals, beverages, and desserts. Some Muslims eat a particular dish called haleem (chicken soup with lentils). Some families listen to nasheeds (Islamic songs). Children also receive gifts, such as money.

In addition, to honor Prophet Abraham's act of sacrifice, Muslims who can afford it usually offer sheep, goat, cow or camel as a symbol of sacrifice. Approximately one third of the meat is given to the poor. The rest is shared with family and friends.

Printed in the United States
by Baker & Taylor Publisher Services